AAT

Management Accounting: Budgeting
Pocket Notes

These Pocket Notes supports study for the following AAT qualifications:
AAT Professional Diploma in Accounting – Level 4
AAT Level 4 Diploma in Business Skills
AAT Professional Diploma in Accounting at SCQF Level 8
Certificate: Accounting (Level 5 AATSA)

British library cataloguing-in-publication data

A catalogue record for this book is available from the British Library.

Published by:
Kaplan Publishing UK
Unit 2 The Business Centre
Molly Millars Lane
Wokingham
Berkshire
RG41 2QZ

ISBN 978-1-78415-612-1

© Kaplan Financial Limited, 2016

Printed and bound in Great Britain.

CONTENTS

Preface

These Pocket Notes contain the key points you need to know for the exam, presented in a unique visual way that makes revision easy and effective.

Written by experienced lecturers and authors, these Pocket Notes break down content into manageable chunks to maximise your concentration.

Quality and accuracy are of the utmost importance to us so if you spot an error in any of our products, please send an email to mykaplanreporting@kaplan.com with full details, or follow the link to the feedback form in MyKaplan.

Our Quality Co-ordinator will work with our technical team to verify the error and take action to ensure it is corrected in future editions.

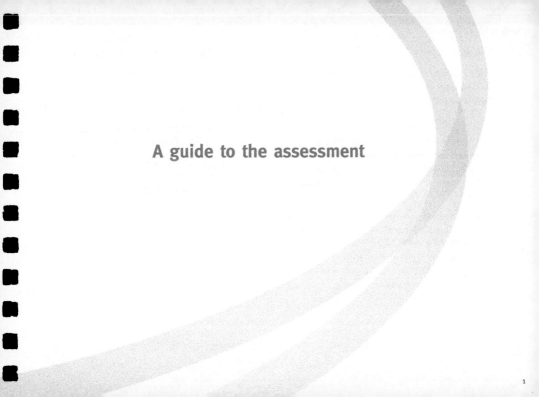

A guide to the assessment

The assessment

MABU is the management accounting unit studied on the Professional Diploma in Accounting qualification.

Examination

Management Accounting: Budgeting is assessed by means of a partially computer/ partially human marked computer based assessment. The CBA will last for 2 hours 30 minutes and consist of 8 tasks.

In any one assessment, students may not be assessed on all content, or on the full depth or breadth of a piece of content. The content assessed may change over time to ensure validity of assessment, but all assessment criteria will be tested over time.

Learning outcomes and weighting

1.	Prepare forecasts of income and expenditure	10%
2.	Prepare budgets	35%
3.	Demonstrate how budgeting can improve organisational performance	35%
4.	Report budgetary information to management in a clear and appropriate format.	20%
Total		100%

Pass mark

To pass a unit assessment, students need to achieve a mark of 70% or more.

This unit contributes 15% of the total amount required for the Professional Diploma in Accounting qualification.

1

Responsibility centres and the behavioural aspects of budgeting

- Behavioural aspects of budgeting.
- Responsibility centres.

Behavioural aspects of budgeting

Target setting and motivation

Targets will assist motivation and appraisal if they are at the right level.

- Too hard and people give up.
- Too easy and people won't try hard enough.

An ideal target should be slightly above the anticipated performance level.

Targets should be:

- Communicated in advance.
- Dependent on factors controllable by the individual.
- Based on quantifiable factors.
- Linked to appropriate rewards and penalties.
- Chosen carefully to ensure goal congruence.
- Challenging but achievable.

Participation is generally agreed to help.

Participation

Top-down budgeting (non-participative)

A budget which is set without allowing the ultimate budget holder to have the opportunity to participate in the budgeting process.

Bottom-up budgeting (participative)

A system of budgeting in which budget holders have the opportunity to participate in setting their own budgets.

Advantages of participative budgets	Disadvantages of participative budgets
1. Increased motivation.	1. Senior managers may resent loss of control.
2. Should contain better information, especially in a fast-moving or diverse business.	2. Bad decisions from inexperienced managers.
3. Increases managers' understanding and commitment.	3. Budgets may not be in line with corporate objectives.
4. Better communication.	4. Budget preparation is slower and disputes can arise.
5. Senior managers can concentrate on strategy.	5. Figures may be subject to bias if junior managers either try to impress or set easily achievable targets (budgetary slack).
	6. Certain environments may preclude participation, e.g. sales manager may be faced with long-term contracts already agreed.

Responsibility centres

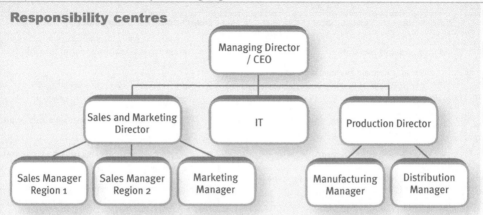

The entire organisation should be divided into various responsibility centres. Each responsibility centre is held by a manager or head of the centre, who has been assigned the responsibility for its budget.

Each responsibility centre should be classified into one of the following categories:

1. Revenue and expense centres;

2. Profit centres;

3. Investment centres.

2

Sources of data

- Internal sources of information.
- External sources of information.

Internal sources of information

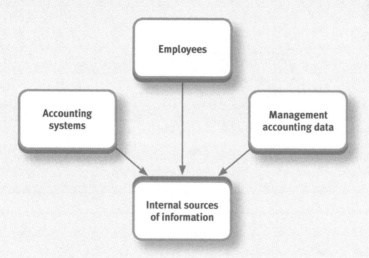

External sources of information

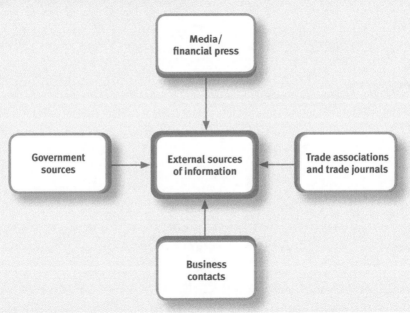

3

Forecasting techniques and the product lifecycle

- Differentiate between forecasts and plans/budgets.
- Time series.
- Sampling.
- Index numbers.

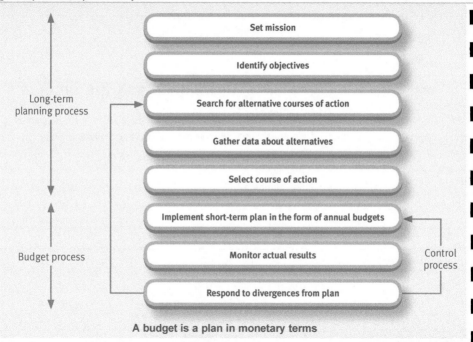

A budget is a plan in monetary terms

Differentiate between forecasts and plans/budgets

Forecast	Budget
The indication of where the business is actually going	A plan for where a business wants to go
An expectation of our estimate of what might happen in the future based on historical data and analysis using various assumptions	A deliberate commitment or intent

Time series

The process of forecasting will inevitably involve some analysis of historic data (sales, costs, share prices, etc) in order that future values may be predicted.

A time series is a set of values for some variable (e.g. monthly production) which varies with time.

Time series analysis takes historic data and breaks it down into component parts that are easier to extrapolate (predict future values for). In particular, it will isolate the underlying trend.

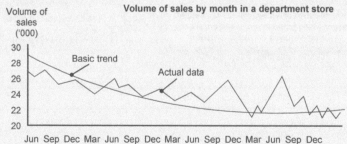

Sampling

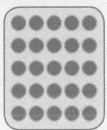

Census approach

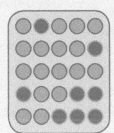

Sampling approach

The census approach examines every item in the population

When sampling is used only a small number of items in the population are examined or tested.

Random sampling
- each item in the population has an equal chance of being included in the sample.

Systematic sampling
- the first item in the sample is chosen using a random number. Thereafter, every nth item in the population is taken to make up the sample.

Stratified sampling
- if the population falls into distinct layers or groups. The population is split into these groups and the sample is then chosen from each group in proportion to the size of the group compared to the total population.

Multistage sampling
- Initially a number of groups or areas are selected randomly. The next stage is to take each group that has been selected and to split them into smaller groups from which again a sample is chosen randomly. This can be done any number of times until the final sample has been chosen.

Index numbers

A time series of figures for costs or income can be easily converted into an index. This is done firstly by choosing a base year and allocating to this year's figure an index of 100. Each subsequent period's figure is then converted into a relevant index number using the formula:

$$\text{Index} = \frac{\text{Current year's figures}}{\text{Base year's figures}}$$

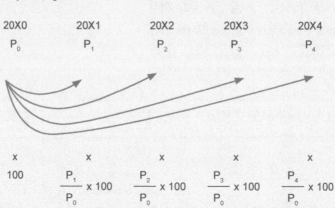

20X0	20X1	20X2	20X3	20X4
P_0	P_1	P_2	P_3	P_4

x	x	x	x	x
100	$\dfrac{P_1}{P_0} \times 100$	$\dfrac{P_2}{P_0} \times 100$	$\dfrac{P_3}{P_0} \times 100$	$\dfrac{P_4}{P_0} \times 100$

In the exam

The budget committee has set the sales volume growth and pricing assumptions for years 2, 3, 4 and 5 in the form of indices. Complete the sales revenue forecast below.

Do not show decimals. Round each figure to the nearest whole number.

	Year 1	Year 2	Year 3	Year 4	Year 5
Sales volume index	130	131	132	133	134
Sales price index	112	115	120	125	130

Sales revenue	Actual Year 1 £	Forecast Year 2 £	Forecast Year 3 £	Forecast Year 4 £	Forecast Year 5 £
At year 1 prices	384,000				
At expected prices					

Solution

To calculate the sales revenue forecast for Year 2 at Year 1 prices, we take the sales revenue for Year 1 and divide it by its sales volume index of 130:

£348,000 / 130 = £2,676.92 (leave this number in your calculator)

We then multiply this by the Year 2 volume index of 131 so £2,676.92 x 131 = £386,954

To calculate the sales revenue forecast for Year 2 at expected prices, we take the sales revenue just calculated of £386,954, divide that by the Year 1 price index of 112 and multiply the result by the Year 2 sales price index of 115:

(£386,954 / 112) * 115 = £397,319

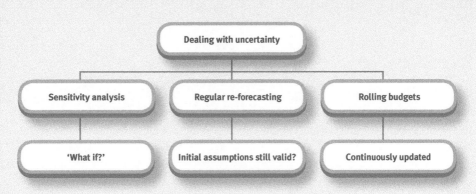

4

Dealing with fixed overheads

- Absorption of overheads.
- Activity-based costing.

Allocation

Where the indirect cost is borne entirely by one cost centre, the entire cost is allocated to that cost centre.

Definition

Apportionment

Where the indirect cost is shared by more than one cost centre, the cost is apportioned between the cost centre.

Definition

Absorption

Absorption is the technique of relating a cost centre's indirect costs to the units produced by the cost centre.

Definition

Overheads arise solely in a particular cost centre. The salary of a supervisor

Key Point

working exclusively in the assembly cost centre would, for example, be treated as an overhead and would be allocated to the assembly cost centre.

Overheads may relate to several cost centres – for example, rent, rates and

Key Point

heating costs. Overheads which relate to several cost centres are shared out or apportioned between the relevant cost centres on the most appropriate basis.

Type of cost	Basis of apportionment
Maintenance	Number of hours worked/machine time
Insurance of machinery	Net book value of machinery
Rent and rates	Floor space occupied (m^2)
Lighting and heating	Volume occupied (m^3)

Arbitrary nature of overhead apportionment

Overhead costs apportioned to different cost centres are simply the result of using a particular basis to share out the overall overheads of a business. If different bases had been chosen then the amounts apportioned to different cost centres would have been different, i.e. the overhead costs are shared out on an arbitrary basis.

Absorption of overheads

Key Point

Having collected all overheads in the production cost centres via overhead allocation, apportionment and reapportionment, the total overhead must be charged to the output of production cost centres. The charging of overhead costs to costs units is called **overhead absorption**.

Absorption rate bases

Various overhead absorption rates exist and the most suitable one should be selected. The use of an absorption rate per unit is for one-product businesses but the following bases may be more appropriate for a multi-product business:

- Absorption rate per direct labour hour.
- Absorption rate per direct machine hour.

Direct labour hour rates are commonly used in labour-intensive production whereas direct machine hour rates are commonly used in machine-intensive production.

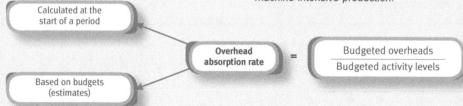

Calculated at the start of a period

Based on budgets (estimates)

$$\text{Overhead absorption rate} = \frac{\text{Budgeted overheads}}{\text{Budgeted activity levels}}$$

Example

Overhead absorption rates

Martin Ltd estimates that the total factory costs for the coming year will be as follows:

	£
Direct materials	40,000
Direct wages	60,000
Prime cost	100,000
Factory overhead	30,000
Total factory cost	130,000

The factory will produce 10,000 units of a variety of different products.

It is anticipated that during the year there will be 30,000 direct labour hours worked and 15,000 machine hours.

Rate per unit $= \dfrac{\text{Budgeted overheads}}{\text{Budgeted production}}$

$= \dfrac{£30,000}{10,000 \text{ units}} = £3 \text{ per unit}$

Rate per direct labour hour

$= \dfrac{\text{Budgeted overheads}}{\text{Budgeted direct labour hours}}$

$= \dfrac{£30,000}{30,000 \text{ hours}} = £1 \text{ per hour}$

Rate per machine hour

$= \dfrac{\text{Budgeted overheads}}{\text{Budgeted machine hours}}$

$= \dfrac{£30,000}{15,000 \text{ hours}} = £2 \text{ per hour}$

Activity based costing (ABC)

The mechanics of ABC

Step 1 Identify major activities.

Step 2 Identify appropriate cost drivers.

Step 3 Collect costs into pools based upon the activities (note: this is usually done for you in a question/task).

Step 4 Charge costs to units of production based on cost driver rate.

$$\text{Cost driver rate} = \frac{\text{Cost pool}}{\text{Level of cost drivers}}$$

Examples

*   Machine costs could be charged using machine hours.

*   Quality control costs could be charged using number of inspections.

*   Set-up costs could be charged using number of set-ups.

Benefits and Limitations of ABC

Benefits

1. Provides more accurate product line costings.

2. Is flexible enough to analyse costs by cost objects other than products, such as processes, areas of managerial responsibility and customers.

3. Provides meaningful financial (periodic cost driver rates) and non-financial (periodic cost driver volumes) measures.

4. Aids identification and understanding of cost behaviour and thus has the potential to improve cost estimation.

5. Provides a more logical, acceptable and comprehensible basis for costing work.

Limitations

1. Little evidence to date that ABC improves corporate profitability.

2. ABC information is historic and internally orientated and therefore lacks direct relevance for future strategic decisions.

3. Practical problems such as cost driver selection.

4. Its novelty is questionable. It may be viewed as simply a rigorous application of conventional costing procedures.

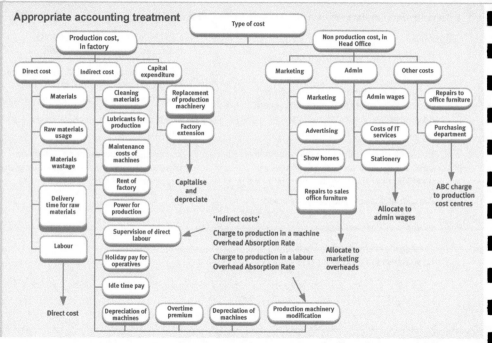

Appropriate accounting treatment

Type of cost

Production cost, in factory

Non production cost, in Head Office

Production cost, in factory:
- Direct cost
  - Materials
  - Raw materials usage
  - Materials wastage
  - Delivery time for raw materials
  - Labour
    → Direct cost
- Indirect cost
  - Cleaning materials
  - Lubricants for production
  - Maintenance costs of machines
  - Rent of factory
  - Power for production
  - Supervision of direct labour
  - Holiday pay for operatives
  - Idle time pay
  - Depreciation of machines
  - Overtime premium
  - Depreciation of machines
  - Production machinery modification
- Capital expenditure
  - Replacement of production machinery
  - Factory extension
    → Capitalise and depreciate

'Indirect costs'

Charge to production in a machine Overhead Absorption Rate

Charge to production in a labour Overhead Absorption Rate

Non production cost, in Head Office:
- Marketing
  - Marketing
  - Advertising
  - Show homes
  - Repairs to sales office furniture
    → Allocate to marketing overheads
- Admin
  - Admin wages
  - Costs of IT services
  - Stationery
    → Allocate to admin wages
- Other costs
  - Repairs to office furniture
  - Purchasing department
    → ABC charge to production cost centres

5

Preparing budgets: the planning phase

- Budget preparation.
- Functional budgets.
- Limiting factors.
- Cash budgets.

Budget preparation

Stages in budget preparation

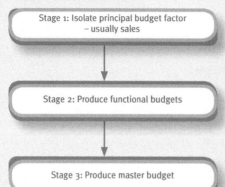

Stage 1: Isolate principal budget factor
– usually sales

Stage 2: Produce functional budgets

Stage 3: Produce master budget

Functional budgets

Typical steps

```
        ┌─────────────────┐
        │  Sales forecast │
        └─────────────────┘
                 │
                 │  Adjust for inventory
                 │  of finished goods
                 ▼
        ┌─────────────────┐
        │   Production    │
        │     budget      │
        └─────────────────┘
          │      │      │
    ┌─────┘      │      └─────┐
    ▼            ▼            ▼
┌─────────┐ ┌─────────┐ ┌─────────┐
│Materials│ │Overhead │ │ Labour  │
│ usage   │ │ budget  │ │utilisa- │
│ budget  │ │         │ │  tion   │
│         │ │         │ │ budget  │
└─────────┘ └─────────┘ └─────────┘
    │                        │
    │ Adjust for inventory   │
    │ of materials           │
    ▼                        ▼
┌─────────┐            ┌─────────┐
│Materials│            │ Labour  │
│purchases│            │  cost   │
│inventory│            │ budget  │
│ budget  │            │         │
└─────────┘            └─────────┘
```

Typical calculations

- **Budgeted production = Forecast sales + closing inventory of finished goods − opening inventory of finished goods.**

- **Materials Usage = Usage per unit x units produced.**

- **Materials purchases budget = forecast materials usage + closing inventory of materials − opening inventory of materials.**

- If dealing with more than one product, keep them separate (side by side in workings) except when producing the materials purchases budget. Here you will need to aggregate the material requirements for both products together.

For the materials budget you'll need to know:

- the amount used per unit of finished goods
- opening and closing inventory of materials
- any allowance for wastage of materials
- the purchase price per unit of material.

Total materials purchases and costs in a month (assuming 5% wastage) is shown here.

	Units (litres,kg, metres)	
Materials for production	M	95%
Add: Wastage M x (5/95)	X	5%
Materials usage	X	100%
Add: closing inventory	X	
Less: opening inventory	-X	
Purchases	Q	
Purchase price per unit	$P	
Purchase cost Q x $P	$X	

Complications

Opening and closing inventories

A business needs a **production budget** as a quantitative expression of its operational plan.

To prepare this, it needs a format for the budget document to be filled in by the Accounting Technician. It also needs information about opening and closing inventory levels from the Production Director.

Production budget	Quantity in units	
	January	February
Opening inventory at the start of the month	4000	3500
Production in month	5500	4800
Sub-total	**9500**	**8300**
Sales in month (units)	6000	4400
Closing inventory at the end of the month	3500	3900

Production required for the month = Sales quantity + Closing inventory quantity - Opening Inventory quantity.

For each month, closing inventory is usually a percentage of the next month's sales. It may also be expressed as the number of days' sales to be held.

Complications

Wastage of completed units

The key here is to adjust in the production budget.

> **Example**
>
> In September a firm plans to sell 161 units. It has 20 units of opening inventory, wants 30 units of closing inventory and typically finds that 5% of units made fail quality control.
>
> How many units of production should be planned?
>
> **Solution**
>
> | | |
> |---|---|
> | Sales | 161 |
> | Less: opening inventory | (20) |
> | Plus: closing inventory | 30 |
> | Production of good units needed | 171 |
> | Production budget = 171/0.95 | **180** |

Wastage of raw materials

This is very similar to wastage of completed units except that the adjustment is made to materials usage.

> **Example**
>
> Continuing the above example, each unit of output uses 2kg of material. 40% of materials input into the production process are wasted. Determine the materials usage budget?
>
> **Solution**
>
> | | |
> |---|---|
> | Production budget | 180 units |
> | Material content of production output (180 x 2) | 360kg |
> | Materials usage budget (i.e. input) = 360/0.6 | 600kg |

For the **labour budget** you'll need to know:

- the hours spent used per unit
- any allowance for inefficiency of labour
- the number of basic hours available
- the rate of pay per basic hour
- the rate of pay for overtime.

Total labour hours and cost in a month (assuming 5% inefficiency) is shown here.

	Hours/$	
Labour for production	L	95%
Add: Inefficiency L x 5 /95	X	5%
Labour hours needed	H	100%
Basic hours available	B	
Overtime hours needed	O	H-8
Basic rate	$R	
Basic hours cost B x $R	$X	
Overtime rate	$P	
Overtime hours cost O x $P	$X	

Wages

The two complications that occur with wages are overtime and minimum guaranteed wages. The key is to compare the labour utilisation with the limits for overtime and guarantees.

Example

Z plc pays its workforce \$8/hr with overtime at time-and-a-half when an individual works more than 50 hours in a week. There is also an agreement that the weekly wage should not fall below \$240 (i.e. 30 hours' worth).

In October the following work was planned for a particular employee. Calculate the wages for the month.

Week	1	2	3	4
Hours	35	40	25	55

Solution

Week	1	2	3	4
Hours	35	40	25	55
Hours paid @\$8	35	40	30	50
Hours paid @\$12	0	0	0	5
Total wages	**280**	**320**	**240**	**460**

For the **machine hours** budget you'll need to know the quantities of

Product	Units produced	Hours per unit	Hours required
A	X	X	X
B	X	X	X
C	X	X	X
Total machine hours required			X
Factory machine hours available = number of machines x maximum hours for each			X
Additional machine hours required			X
			Quantity
Number of machines to hire (round this figure up) = additional hours / maximum hours per machine			X

Limiting factors

The level of activity at which a business can operate will very seldom be unlimited. Limitations may be imposed, for example, by:

- market demand for its products or services;
- the number of skilled employees available;
- the availability of material supplies;
- the space available either as a working area or for the storage of goods;
- the amount of cash or credit facilities available to finance the business.

Where one particular limitation is of major importance it may be necessary to budget for that item first and to construct the rest of the budget around it. the item concerned may be referred to as the principal budget factor or key factor.

Quite commonly, the rate of growth in sales is the principal budget factor and this would have to be forecast before any other budget plans were made.

It is essential to identify the principal budget factor and any other limiting factors at an early stage in the budgeting process so that management may consider whether:

- it is possible to overcome the limitation which they impose (e.g. by finding new markets for sales or by obtaining alternative supplies or substitute raw materials);
- the limitations imposed must be accepted and the business's budgets must be produced within those limitations.

If a business makes more than one product and does not have enough resources to make all it can sell of all products, it must decide which one(s) to produce in full and which to produce in part. This is done based on **contribution per unit of limiting factor**.

Example

A business makes two products X and Y using the same materials, labour and machine capacity. It keeps no inventory of finished goods. The sales price, sales demand and standard cost of each unit, and current availability of resources, are set out as follows:

Table 1	Product X	Product Y	Current availability
Sales demand in months (units)	1,500	3,000	
	$	$	
Selling price per unit	33.00	63.00	
Materials: 0.75kg / 2kg at £3 per kg	2.25	6.00	7,200 kg
Labour: 1.25hrs / 2.5hrs at £12 per hour	15.00	30.00	9,000 hours
Machine time 0.5hrs / 1 hr at £15 per hour	7.50	15.00	4,000 hours
Contribution per unit	8.25	12.00	

After identifying labour as the limiting factor, the completed production budget is provided as follows:

Table 2: Production budget usage for sales demand	Product X	Product Y	Total required
Materials (kg)	1,125	6,000	7,125
Labour (hours)	1,875	7,500	9,375
Machine time (hours)	750	3,000	3,750
Contribution per unit of limiting factor (labour) (£)	6.60	4.80	
Production (units)	1,500	2,850	

Production of X uses 1,500 x 1,875 hours

Remaining hours available = 9,000 - 1,875 = 7,125

Production of Y: 7,125/2.5 = 2,850 units

Cash budgets

Cash inflows	Cash outflows

Cash inflows

Revenue receipts
- cash sales
- receipts from credit customers

Capital receipts
- taking out a loan
- issue of more shares
- sale of non-current assets

Cash outflows

Revenue payments
- cash purchases
- payments to credit suppliers
- wage payments
- payment of bills/expenses

Capital payments
- repayment of loans
- purchase of non-current assets

Tax payments
- dividends/loan interest/ drawings

CBT focus

In a simulation if you are preparing a cash budget you will have to recognise the appropriate cash flows to be included, based on SFP and IS movements. However in many simulations you are given a pro-forma for the cash budget which will indicate which figures are relevant.

6

Preparing budgets: the control phase

- Cost classifications.
- Cost behaviour.
- Splitting semi-variable costs.
- Flexed budgets.
- Flexible budgets.
- Materials variances.
- Labour variances.
- Interdependence of variances.
- Variance investigation.
- Reasons for variances.
- Basic methods of budgeting.

Cost classifications

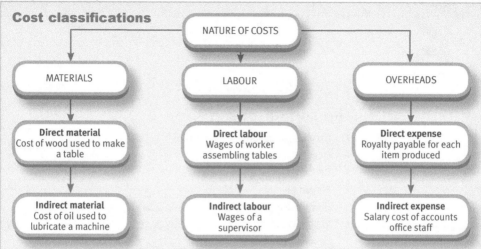

Indirect costs are also knows as overheads.

Production indirect costs are indirect costs involved in the production process, e.g. supervisor salary costs.

Non-production indirect costs are indirect costs involved in converting finished goods into revenue, e.g. administrative staff costs.

Cost behaviour

A **variable cost** increases as the level of activity increases.	A **fixed cost** does not increase as the level of activity increases.

Graph of variable cost

Graph of fixed cost

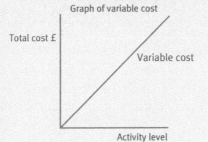

Total cost £

Variable cost

Activity level

Total cost £

Fixed cost
(or period cost)

Activity level

Examples of variable costs:

Direct materials

Direct labour

Examples of fixed costs:

Business rates

Management salaries

A **semi-variable cost** is one that contains both fixed and variable elements.

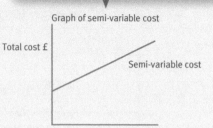

Graph of semi-variable cost

Total cost £

Semi-variable cost

Activity level

Semi-variable costs are also known as **semi-fixed costs** or **mixed costs**.

Examples of semi-variable costs:

Electricity costs – standing charge (fixed cost)
– cost per unit used (variable cost)

Salesman's salary – basic (fixed) + bonus (variable)

A **stepped cost** is one that remains fixed over a certain range of activity, but increases if activity increases beyond that level.

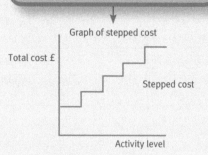

Graph of stepped cost

Total cost £

Stepped cost

Activity level

Examples of stepped costs:

Inventory storage costs

Supervisor salaries

Splitting semi-variable costs

High/low method

If a semi-variable cost is incurred, it is often necessary to estimate the fixed and variable elements of the cost for the purposes of budgeting. The costs can be split using the **High/low Method.**

$$\text{Variable cost per unit (VC)} = \frac{\text{Change in total cost}}{\text{Change in level of production}}$$

Fixed cost = Total cost − (VC x units produced)

Flexed budgets

- For variances to be meaningful and appropriate for use as decision-making tools, a **flexed budget** should be prepared to take into account the change between the budgeted levels of activity (sales and production) and the actual levels.

	Budget	Flexed budget	Actual
Sales volume	100 units	90 units	90 units
Sales value	£1,000	£900	£990
Variable costs	£500	£450	£495
Fixed costs	£200	£200	£210
Profit	£300	£250	£285

Flexible budgets

A **fixed** budget contains information on costs and revenue for one level of activity. A **flexible** budget shows the same information, but for a number of different levels of activity.

	Low	Normal	High
Activity level	80,000 units	100,000 units	120,000 units
Revenue	£3,200,000	£4,000,000	£4,800,000
Variable costs	£1,440,000	£1,800,000	£2,160,000
Fixed costs	£300,000	£300,000	£300,000
Profit	£1,460,000	£1,900,000	£2,340,000

A **flexible** budget model makes it possible to quickly amend the line items in the event of some unforeseen complication. For example, should sales volume suddenly drop, affecting the amount of generated revenue, the flexible format makes it easy to quickly change the amounts associated with specific line items to reflect the new set of circumstances.

The ability to quickly adjust a flexible budget to take into account changes in output levels or shifts in income means that a business can move quickly to meet the new circumstances. By contrast, a fixed budget, that is based on a single set of projections and allows no room for adjustments without going through a complicated approval process, wastes valuable time and money that could be used more efficiently.

Materials variances

1 Materials price variance

The material price variance is calculated compared to what we expected to pay, so that we can work out whether we have paid too much or too little for our materials.

We always use the **Purchased quantity** in the calculation and we compare the Actual price paid and the **Standard** (expected) price.

> **Formula:**
>
> Actual quantity purchased × Actual price
> V
> Actual quantity purchased × Standard price
>
> Materials price variance   £X F/ A

We can also use what we call the Did and Should method to work out an answer.

x units did cost	£X
x units should have cost @ £x	£X
Variance	£X F/A

2 Materials Usage variance

The materials usage variance is calculated so that we can work out whether we have used too much or too little material to manufacture our goods in the period.

We always use the Used quantity of material in the calculation, and we compare the Actual amount of materials used with the Standard (expected) amount of materials that we should use to make the actual volume of goods in the period (the activity level.)

Formula:	
Actual quantity used × Standard price	
V	
Standard quantity used for actual production × Standard price	
Materials usage variance	£X F/A

We can also use what we call the Did and Should method to work out an answer.

x units did use	x	kgs
x units should have used @ 2 sq metres per box	x	kgs
	x	kgs
Multiplied by the standard (expected) price	*£x	
So variance is	£X	

Labour variances

1 Labour rate variance

The labour rate variance is calculated so that we can work out whether or not we have paid the correct hourly rate to the direct labour employees. We always use the total hours paid and we compare the Actual hourly rate paid and the standard (expected) hourly rate

---

Formula:

Actual labour hours paid × Actual rate
V
Actual labour hours paid × Standard rate

Labour rate variance   £X F/A

When calculating the labour rate variance we could again use what we call the Did and Should method to work out the answer.

x hours did cost	£X
x hours should have cost @ £X per hour	£X
Variance	£X

2 Labour efficiency variance

The labour efficiency variance is calculated so that we can work out whether we have used too much or too little labour to manufacture our goods in the period.

We always use the worked quantity of hours and we compare the actual number of hours worked and the standard (expected) number of hours that we should work to make the volume of goods in the period (the activity level).

Formula:	
Actual hours worked × Standard rate	
V	
Standard hours worked for actual production × Standard rate	
Labour efficiency variance	£X F/A

We can use the Did and Should method to calculate the labour efficiency also.

X units did use	X hours
X units should have used @ x minutes per box	X hours
	X hours
Multiplied by the standard (expected) rate	× £X per hour
so variance is	£X

3   Idle time variance

The idle time variance is calculated as the difference between the direct labour hours paid and the direct labour hours worked. It is a balancing figure and it is always adverse. It is always calculated using the standard (expected) hourly rate.

> Actual hours paid × Standard rate
> V
> Actual hours worked × Standard rate

Hours paid for	X hours
Hours worked	X hours
	X hours
Multiplied by the standard (expected) rate	× £X per hour
so variance is	£X F / A

Interdependence of variances

The cause of a variance may affect another variance in a corresponding or opposite way.

For example, workers trying to improve productivity (favourable labour efficiency variance) might become careless and waste more material (adverse material usage variance.)

Variance investigation

Variance calculations are just the starting point. Next, management need to decide which variances are worth investigating. To do this they will consider the following.

- How big is the variance?
  - Absolute size
  - Relative size as a % of standard
  - Overall trend
- Is it favourable or adverse?
- Possible reasons for it
  - Planning errors
  - Measurement problems
  - Random factors
  - Operational issues
- Controllability
- Cost v benefit of investigation

- Likelihood of a problem, based on past experience
- The overall picture given by all the variances

Management will seek to assign responsibility for the variances so they can be investigated further.

Reasons for variances

Variance		Possible causes
Materials:	Price	Bulk discounts
		Different suppliers/ Different materials
		Unexpected delivery costs
		Different buying procedures
	Usage	Different quality material
		Theft, obsolescence, deterioration
		Different quality of staff
		Different mix of material
		Different batch sizes and trim loss
Labour:	Rate	Different class of labour
		Excessive overtime
		Productivity bonuses
		National wage negotiations
		Union action

Variance		Possible causes
	Efficiency	Different levels of skill
		Different working conditions
		The learning effect
		Lack of supervision
		Works to rule
		Machine breakdowns
		Lack of material
		Lack of orders
		Strikes (if paid)
		Too long over coffee breaks
Overhead:	Price	Change in nature of overhead
		Unforeseen price changes
	Volume	Excessive idle time
		Increase in workforce

Basic methods of budgeting

Incremental (historic)

- Starts with previous period's budget or actual results and adds (or subtracts) an incremental amount to cover inflation and other known changes.

- Suitable for stable businesses, where costs are not expected to change significantly.

- There should be good cost control and limited discretionary costs.

Zero-based budgeting

- Requires cost element to be specifically justified, as though the activities to which the budget relates were being undertaken for the first time.

- Without approval, the budget allowance is zero.

- Suitable for allocating resources in areas were spend is discretionary.

Priority-based budgeting

- A competitively ranked listing of high to low priority discrete bids for "decision packages."
  - All activities are re-evaluated each time a budget is set.
  - Does not require a zero assumption

Activity-based budgeting

- Preparing budgets using overhead costs from activity based costing methodology.

7

Preparing budgets: the decision-making stage

- Types of standard.
- Performance Indicators.

Types of Standard

Performance standard	Detail
Ideal	Based on perfect conditions
	Allows for no inefficiencies, or wastage, or idle time.
	Employees can become de-motivated.
Attainable	Some allowance is made for wastage and inefficiencies
	Realistic but challenging target.
Current	Based on current working conditions.
	Does not attempt to improve on current levels of efficiency.
Basic	Kept unaltered over a long period of time.
	May be out of date.
	Used to show change in performance over time.

Performance indicators

The examiner has grouped these measures into four areas:

1 **Quality** indicators such as reject rates;

2 **Efficiency indicators,** such as the number of products made per labour hour, or idle time ratios;

3 **Capacity measures,** such as machine utilisation ratios (or 'asset utilisation' ratios);

4 **Simple financial measures** such as the average selling price, profit percentage of sales revenue, material cost of material per unit of purchase, labour rate per hour, cost per unit of production and sales and cost variances.

Index

W